SHOOTING STARS

Osprey Colour Series

SHOOTING STARS

LOCKHEED'S LEGENDARY T-BIRD

Michael O'Leary

For Mac Short, who made the T-Bird happen

Published in 1988 by Osprey Publishing Limited
27A Floral Street, London WC2E 9DP
Member company of the George Philip Group

© Michael O'Leary

British Library Cataloguing in Publication Data

O'Leary, Michael
  Shooting stars; Lockheed's legendary T-bird.—(Osprey colour series).
  1. Shooting Stars, T-33 (Training plane)—Pictorial works
  I. Title
  623.74′62
  UG1242.T6

ISBN 0-85045-846-3

Editor Dennis Baldry
Designed by David Tarbutt
Printed in Hong Kong

Title pages The National Guard Bureau's airplanes have always been very highly polished (see the NGB's Douglas Invader on page 40 of the author's *Bombing Iron*, another Osprey Colour Series book) and T-33A-1-LO s/n 53-5226 is such an example. Lockheed produced 5691 T-Birds in 28 contract batches over a period of eleven Fiscal Years. Canadair built 656 CL-30 Silver Stars with the R-R Nene engine (see relevant chapter, page 62) and Kawasaki built 210 under-licence in Japan

Michael O'Leary (pictured on the right in the back seat of a California Air National Guard T-33) is employed as an editor for a Los Angeles-based group of aviation magazines. In order to create *Shooting Stars*, he has drawn on his extensive file of aircraft photographs as well as visiting several of the units still operating the classic T-Bird.

Aerial photographs in this volume were produced with Nikon cameras using Kodachrome K25 and K64 film.

Special thanks are due to the following individuals who helped make this book on a classic jet trainer possible: Brigadier-General E Ian Patrick, Captain Rodney Ward, Captain Martin Baggeley, the men of VU-33, the men of the Oregon and California Air National Guard, Captain Sally Morger, and Denis J Calvert.

Front cover T-33s of the California Air National Guard and Oregon ANG 'Redhawks' (nearest T-Bird) formate over the Sierras. Although USAF/ANG T-Birds are being retired with Fiscal Year 1988, many third world nations will continue to operate the type for many years to come—until decreasing serviceability and lack of spare parts force their retirement. With over two dozen civilian T-Birds operating in the States, the type will almost certainly remain active into the 21st century

Back cover Faded and weathered from several years of desert storage at Davis-Monthan AFB, T-33B BuNo 137950 is prepared for a return to service during 1970. Many ex-USN T-33Bs were put back into flying shape by the USAF and turned over to governments friendly to the United States. ATU-205 stood for Advanced Training Unit

Foreword

Few aircraft have survived so well and been so loved as the Lockheed T-33 series. Affectionately known as the 'T-Bird' and occasionally as the 'T-Bag' or 'Lockheed Racer', the T-33 was ubiquitous for thirty years. Almost every military pilot in the Western world has flown in or with the aircraft and the type has worn the colours of many nations. Now, almost suddenly, this wonderful aircraft has become a rarity.

Conceived by Lockheed engineers to provide special jet training for pilots destined for the P-80 single-seat fighter, the T-Bird was so successful that over 7000 were built. Despite its 1940s' lineage and its 1950s' production, the aircraft has an enviable combination of performance and economy. To its admirers, the 'old girl' has a beauty all her own and, like a first love, always will.

Straight wings, with ungainly tip tanks, a less-than-powerful World War Two-type tail and rather plain features characterize this aircraft but there is a gracefulness in every line. Curves abound, as befits a thing of beauty, no pointed nose or sharp angles typical of supersonic machines—she was not designed for speed, but for reliability and handling qualities as a trainer.

Never an easy aircraft to fly, the T-Bird continuously challenges and demands its pilots to pay attention and to be precise—but with a gentle touch. Designed for flight at 20,000 feet, the T-Bird without tip tanks is a delightfully responsive and capable trainer. Fully loaded, with tip tanks and above 30,000 feet, the aircraft will deliver $2\frac{1}{2}$ to 3 hours of butt-numbing experience on the hard 'bang' seat, while giving the pilot the feeling he is balancing on the end of a needle.

Although a day VFR aircraft in concept, the trainer rapidly demanded a night and all-weather capability. Being a neutrally stable aircraft, without autopilot and with a basic panel, the T-33 can be a handful in rough and stormy weather. Attention is one thing this lady demands.

Instructing student pilots in the T-Bird can be a weight-losing experience as well. With those large tip tanks flailing around, an instructor dare not even blink. Punishment, however, is something the aircraft takes well, and the efforts of the most errant students often failed to ground her.

Of the thousands built, only a few hundred T-Birds remain. Canada's air force plans to retain over sixty until the turn of the century, and several air forces throughout the world probably will double that number. If the Boeing Skyfox appeals to customers, the lady will live on in new finery.

To those of us who grew up with the T-Bird, trained today's pilots and still fly her, the T-Bird will always evoke deep-down feelings of excitement and pleasure. No matter her age, she still titillates and beckons tantalizingly, rewarding only the most skillful, the most patient. To know her is to love her forever. She is a captivating mistress *par excellence*.

Brigadier-General Ian Patrick
Canadian Forces
CFB Winnipeg
November 1987

Brigadier-General Ian Patrick is pictured on the contents page (right)

Contents

USAF/ANG stand down

On 22 March 1948, aviation history was made—albeit in fairly quiet fashion—when Lockheed test pilot Tony LeVier lifted the TP-80C off the runway at Van Nuys, California, for the aircraft's first flight. The airplane, basically a P-80 fighter modified to two-seat dual-control configuration, was known variously as the Lockheed Trainer, Shooting Star (merely a continuation of the P-80's name), or, perhaps more universally, as the T-Bird. The prototype TP-80C went on to make aviation history as the most popular jet trainer ever built. After forty years of continuous United States Air Force and Air National Guard service, the T-Bird is finally being retired during Fiscal 1988. To commemorate this event for *Shooting Stars*, the California and Oregon ANGs combined forces to create a very special T-Bird flight on 5 October 1987. Four T-Birds were launched from Fresno, California, home of the 194th Fighter Interceptor Group, and consisted of two CA ANG aircraft (camera ship flown by Bill Gore, and 586 flown by Bob Crow) and two OR ANG 'Redhawks' T-Birds (667 flown by Greg Dykes and 943 piloted by Rich Hayes)

T-Birds in echelon. Our 5 October 1987 formation was unique in the fact that it brought three different colour schemes into one photograph. The California ANG aircraft is polished natural metal while one of the Redhawks' aircraft is overall light grey and the other is unique for being the only ANG T-Bird to carry Egyptian One camouflage—giving the old trainer a rather hi-tech look. Lockheed's rugged trainer was ordered into production during the early part of 1948 when 20 TP-80Cs were contracted. The designation of the aircraft was changed to TF-80C on 11 June 1948 and to T-33A on 5 May 1949

Preceding pages To create the two-seat trainer variant of the P-80 Shooting Star, Lockheed engineers added a 38.6 inch plug in front of the wing and a 12 inch plug aft of the wing. This gave ample room for a fully instrumented dual-control tandem cockpit. Oddly, the increased length and longer canopy helped streamline the plane and the trainer was actually a bit faster than the fighter! Lockheed had developed the trainer with its own funds (one million 1947 dollars, a pretty good bargain) and was to reap huge rewards over the production life of the aircraft. Tony LeVier recalls designer Kelly Johnson stating, 'The government needs a jet trainer. Right now they don't want it but they're going to get it, and I think they will like it.' Our ANG T-Bird formation is seen over the rugged Sierras, nearly forty years after the prototype T-Bird's first flight

The very flat, dull two-tone grey camouflage scheme carried by 943 is shown to advantage over the parched Sierras—which, when photographed, were experiencing some of the worse drought and fires in modern history. LeVier reported that the new trainer flew 'like an F-80, only faster.' The large canopy was subjected to the pressures of high-speed flight and, on LeVier's third hop, this fact nearly cost his life. He was demonstrating the airplane to USAF brass when the canopy tore off during a high-speed pass but the test pilot managed to recover even though his helmet had been ripped off by the force of the airflow. The canopy mounts were modified

The Redhawks' unusually camouflaged T-Bird is held in tight formation by Rich Hayes. S/n 53-5943 is the personal mount of Brigadier-General C Sams of the Oregon ANG. There is a great deal of regret among ANG personnel about the demise of the T-Bird by mid-1988 since there really is not a comparable replacement aircraft. There is a slight chance that a few T-Birds will soldier on in American service in specialized roles but the majority of currently serving aircraft will be transferred to nations 'south of the border'

Above The attractive stylized Redhawk insignia carried on the vertical tail of 53-5943. T-Birds were initially fitted with two .50 calibre Browning machine guns in the nose (the P-80 carried six) but, currently, none of the surviving USAF/ANG examples are armed. However, T-Birds being sent 'south' are having this armament re-installed along with the ability to carry 2000 lbs of underwing stores. These aircraft are usually given the designation of AT-33A

Inset The hi-tech radar absorbing camouflage on 943 causes many second looks when the airplane lands at a base away from home. This view shows the stenciled information block to advantage. Note how crew helmets are now adopting the toned-down look

Right S/n 56-1586 with everything down and out while 943 rides shotgun overhead. Polished T-Birds are quite often the pride of individual crew chiefs (but probably not the airmen who spend many hours keeping the aluminium in pristine condition). The inside portion of the wingtip fuel tanks have been painted flat black to minimize glare

Preceding pages (left) The T-Bird formation assumes a classic line-astern formation while the pilots demonstrate their considerable close formation skills. Photo chase pilot Bill Gore formated our T-Bird so close that a Nikkor 18mm lens had to be used for this shot—*no sweat*!

Preceding pages (right) Here's what the rear pit of an ANG T-Bird looks like during flight. As can be seen, there's little evidence of today's hi-tech USAF but that's no problem since the T-Bird performs its mission with a minimum of trouble and in a cost-effective manner

Right Straight up! 586 heads up over the Sierras during the start of a formation loop. The T-Bird is a strong aircraft that is suitable for aerobatics. The first USAF T-Birds were delivered with Allison J33-A-23 engines of 4600 lbs thrust and were a bit underpowered so the 5200 lb thrust J33-A-25 was introduced. Most aircraft were later re-engined with the J33-A-35 that offers 5400 lbs thrust

This page Canopy open to help dissipate the California heat, 586 prepares to take the active at Fresno. The 194th Fighter Interceptor Squadron shares Fresno's Hammer Field with airliners and civilian aircraft, and has been operating T-Birds since September 1954. At the time of our visit, four T-Birds were with the unit and one of these had been with the unit since received as new!

The clean lines of the T-Bird are evident in this view of 586. The 194th has operated a variety of fighter aircraft over the years, including Mustangs, Sabres, Delta Daggers, Delta Darts and, currently, Phantoms in the air defence role. The T-33 entered USAF service in 1948 and remained the USAF's sole jet trainer until 1957 when the Cessna T-37A 'Tweety Bird' was introduced. During its service with the USAF, the T-Bird has performed just about every training role possible

Above Light overall grey paint characterizes most surviving T-Birds. At the time of our photo flight, Redhawks' T-Bird 52-9667 was the oldest operating T-33 in the inventory. This aircraft has its nose radomes painted white rather than the more usual black

Overleaf 667 begins its downwind turn towards Hammer Field prior to landing. Note the underwing pylons. The Redhawks use their T-Birds for dissimilar air combat training and ECM pods are sometimes carried on the pylons. The pylons can support up to 2000 lbs of underwing stores

Above After the flight, the T-Birds are refuelled and Greg Dykes fills out the necessary forms. It's interesting to note that the aircraft is older than the pilot. Greg normally flies a Phantom for the Oregon ANG

Right 586 rolls away from the camera plane. During its period of active training, the T-Bird was used by the 147th Fighter Interceptor Group of the Texas ANG who set up the Jet Instrument School of the ANG and this unit became responsible for instructing all ANG pilots in the fine art of instrument flying

Drones and hacks

With large numbers of T-33s in the government inventory and with an entirely new generation of airborne weapons, a decision was made to convert surplus USAF T-33s to drone configuration. The converted aircraft were given the new designation QT-33A and were assigned to the Pacific Missile Test Center at Point Mugu,

California, on the shore of the Pacific Ocean, and to the Naval Weapons Center at China Lake, in California's high desert. The aircraft were used for targets but were also fully capable of being flown by 'real' pilots rather than electronic signals and sometimes served as observation aircraft or as directors for other drones. With its J33 running, a crew chief makes last minute checks before launching a Pt. Mugu QT-33A in conjunction with a North American QF-86H Sabre, seen in the background, during September 1975

Conversion to QT-33A status was relatively straightforward, the necessary electronics being easily accommodated in the T-Bird's spacious nose and fuselage area. Drone aircraft were supposed to be given an overall scheme of Semi-gloss Fluorescent Yellow Orange but this order was often interpreted quite liberally, with several variants of bright red or dayglo colours being applied to airframes. This well-worn QT-33A is seen awaiting its next mission. Note the non-standard nose probe

Parked on the ramp at a foggy Pt. Mugu, QT-33A BuNo 155988 displays some of the non-standard antennas common to the T-Birds modified as drones (note the pole antenna directly to the rear of the nose gear doors and the one directly in front). The Navy received 252 USAF T-33As for drone conversion

Overleaf Brightly painted in what appears to be International Orange, a clutch of QT-33As shelters near Douglas A-3 'Whales' assigned to the Naval Missile Center at Pt. Mugu. By the time this photograph was taken in November 1972, air-to-air missiles had become highly accurate and the QT-33A fleet would have been depleted very quickly except for the fact that the missiles were usually not carrying warheads and were quite often guided to a near hit, so that the drone could fly again another day. However, it was rare for the drones to survive over a dozen flights

QT-33A BuNo 155948 parked on the ramp at China Lake during a June 1970 display. China Lake is the home for the Naval Weapons Center and testing on new forms of weapons (many often classified) is a daily activity. The QT-33As assigned to China Lake were expended in a violent manner and a visitor to the base can spot several mangled wrecks still sticking out of the desert scrub. Today, QF-86Fs are the drone of choice at China Lake, the T-Birds having been made an extinct species

It's a sad fact but, in this 40th anniversary year for the T-Bird, virtually all of the QT-33As have been destroyed in missile and weapons testing or in accidents (not uncommon in drone operations, especially if the drone has been damaged by a hit and the operator is attempting to recover the airplane). Although never designed for combat, the QT-33As fell victim to some of the world's most sophisticated weapons

Top left Photographed on 21 October 1962, this TV-2D (a pre-September 1962 designation, before the consolidation of USN/USAF aircraft designations, but this aircraft, obviously, had not yet met the attention of the squadron sign painter) was utilized as a drone director for Navy T-Bird drones and other drone aircraft. The Navy modified some of its TV-2 fleet into drone directors and actual drones (TV-2KD/DT-33C). BuNo 141539 wears a faded USN Target Drone Director colour scheme of Engine Grey fuselage, Orange Yellow wings and Fluorescent Red Orange tail and wing stripes. The California sun at Pt. Mugu has had telling effects on the lighter colours

Left Here's BuNo 141539 again, still at Pt. Mugu but photographed on 18 May 1963 after it had received a new paint scheme and redesignation to DT-33B. The tail designation has changed from Pacific Missile Range to Naval Missile Center. Pt. Mugu has always been home to an eclectic collection of aircraft types, as noted by the Skyrays and Demons in the background

Below To the uninitiated, the term 'hack' may have negative connotations. However, to USAF pilots from the 1960s to the present day, 'hack' probably means pleasant memories—and those memories usually evolve around the Lockheed T-33. Since the USAF procured vast quantities of T-Birds and since the training role was being assumed by the newer Cessna T-37s and Northrop T-38s, many T-Birds were released to command units, squadrons, and air bases to use for general transport duties, pilot currency training, fighter and threat simulation, fun flying and just plain hell raising. Once on this level of operation, T-Birds were usually maintained in absolutely pristine condition and were quite often the mounts of commanding officers. This T-33A, photographed during May 1968, exhibits a beautiful polished finish—indicative of many man-hours put in by enlisted men. The T-Bird carries a Strategic Air Command (SAC) band around the fuselage and the insignia of a one-star general on the vertical fin fillet

Below Attractively finished T-33A-5-LO s/n 58-550 was assigned to the 318th Fighter Interceptor Squadron during September 1971. Fighter squadrons have always had plenty of uses for the T-Bird, the airplane being a particularly good target during dissimilar air combat training (DACT). Stressed to 7.5Gs, the T-Bird is a tough aircraft that is hard to 'bend' during practice dogfights

Above Seen parked on a frozen ramp during March 1974 with a row of SAC Boeing B-52Gs in the background, this T-33A was assigned to the 5th Fighter Interceptor Squadron (proudly proclaimed on the gloss black tip tank which also carries the airplane's serial of 58-610, making the aircraft a T-33A-5-LO from one of the last batch of T-Birds built by Lockheed). These hacks quite often carried the parent unit's insignia, as can be seen on the vertical tail. A travel pod is also attached under the fuselage

Left The pilot of T-33A-1-LO s/n 56-1753 prepares to start the Allison J33 prior to a September 1966 mission. Assigned to the 52nd Fighter Interceptor Wing (the unit's 'Seek, Attack, Destroy' insignia is carried on the vertical tail), the T-Bird carries large underwing chaff dispensing pods which were used in conjunction with combat manoeuvres carried out by the unit's fighters. Photographed at Dover AFB

Top left Today, most National Aeronautics and Space Administration (NASA) hacks are relatively modern Northrop T-38 Talons. However, NASA used to have quite a few T-Birds on its active list. This particular T-33A carries standard USAF markings except for the legend NASA 917 on the vertical tail. Photographed during January 1966

Above T-33A-5-LO s/n 52-9658 on the ramp amid the bare wasteland that makes up Nellis AFB on 26 October 1963, a Republic F-84F parked in the background. Nellis, currently home of Red Flag exercises, has always hosted air combat events and this T-Bird, assigned to the 331st Fighter Interceptor Squadron, was undoubtedly visiting such an exercise

Left T-33A-5-LO s/n 58-695 was another T-Bird attractively decked out in Strategic Air Command markings. Lockheed constructed 5691 T-Birds at Burbank and as the training mission was taken over by more modern aircraft, many T-Birds were made available for other units. This particular machine was stationed with the 305th Bomb Wing ('Can Do' badge on the fuselage) and based at Bunker Hill AFB, Indiana, during May 1968 (the base is now Grissom AFB in honour of astronaut Gus Grissom). Highly polished, the small travelling 'suitcase' is attached under the fuselage

Overleaf Very nicely finished T-33A-5-LO s/n 58-565 at Nellis AFB, Nevada, on 26 October 1963. This particular machine was flown by a brigadier-general, as indicated by the two rank stars carried on the vertical tail just under the badge for the 26th Air Division. Markings of interest include the large 'buzz' number (TR was the code assigned to the T-Bird fleet) on the nose and the elaborate fuselage bands. The T-Birds large tip tanks (carrying 230 US gallons and capable of being jettisoned in an emergency) served as good billboards for identifying the T-33's parent unit

Right Freshly arrived at Davis-Monthan AFB for pickling and preservation, T-33A-1-LO s/n 56-1592 shows one last pose of defiance before being sprayed with preservative coating. The T-Bird's life has been so long that some examples have been through this process several times at D-M, being made airworthy and assigned to a new unit or sent to foreign nations friendly to the United States. When seen during July 1971, this T-Bird was finished in the markings of the Air Defense Weapons Center

Bottom right T-33A-5-LO s/n 58-552 at McGuire AFB, New Jersey, during May 1965. The highly polished T-33 sports grey tip tanks identifying the parent unit as the New York Air Defense Sector. The folded white object in the rear cockpit is the instrument flying hood, which is deployed by sliding forward on the lines mounted under the canopy

Below Carrying underwing chaff dispensers and the small fuselage mounted suitcase, T-33A-1-LO s/n 53-5156

Left Surrounded by rows of fellow T-Birds, T-33A-5-LO s/n 53-5203 sits pickled and preserved at Davis-Monthan AFB on 28 December 1962—awaiting either a new assignment or scrapping. Given the early date, this aircraft, which last saw service as a hack with Robins AFB, was probably put back into service when a requirement came along. Note the buzz number placed on the rear fuselage. With replacement of all USAF/ANG T-Birds in Fiscal Year 88, a suitable replacement is not readily available that will have the versatility and flying qualities of the forty-year-old design. Most likely, civilian contracted Learjets will be used by fighter units for DACT missions

Above T-33A-5-LO s/n 58-675 was, when photographed on 9 March 1968, a base hack at Perrin AFB in Texas. When assigned to a particular base rather than a specific unit, T-Birds were mainly employed for quick transportation of ranking officers and for keeping said officers current in their flying duties

Top left The 95th Fighter Interceptor Squadron's rather ghastly squadron insignia of a skull with a top hat and cane is proudly displayed on the vertical tail of T-33A-5-LO s/n 56-1712 at Dover AFB during September 1966. By this time, in order to decrease maintenance, the underside fuselage of many T-Birds was painted gloss grey, making areas difficult to reach easier to clean. The large chaff pods dispersed bursts of what was basically chopped-up aluminium foil and this was used to confuse ground radar as well as the airborne radar carried by intercepting fighter aircraft with whom the T-Birds would practice DACT

The replacement that didn't

Below Lockheed, somewhat startled by the success of its TF-80C/T-33 programme, reasoned that an updated, improved variant would enjoy even more financial success. Whereas the T-33 project was a fairly minimal modification of the F-80, the new project would incorporate many modifications. Started in October 1952 and given Temporary Design Designation L-245, the prototype was unofficially known around Burbank as the T-33B. The airplane would become the T2V-1 (redesignated T-1A during modernization and amalgamation of aircraft designations undertaken by the government on 18 September 1962). T-1A BuNo 144751 was assigned to the United States Marine Corps' H&MS-14 (Headquarters and Maintenance Squadron FOURTEEN, assigned tail code CN) when photographed during October 1968. The T-1A is painted in overall Aircraft Gray

Above The Model L-245 was guided through the initial concept and design phase by Kelly Johnson—creator of so many of Lockheed's record-setting aircraft. Johnson wanted to decrease instructor workload while improving the design's low-speed characteristics. Since the back seat of the T-33 could be a bit of a 'black hole' during approach, Johnson designed the L-245's rear cockpit to be six inches higher than the front seat. Combined with a raised and bulged canopy, the instructor had a much more satisfactory view of the outside world and was able to keep a closer eye on his student. The raised rear seat is seen clearly in this view (note the neatly folded instrument flying hood) of T2V-1 BuNo 144736 during August 1960. The T2V-1 is painted in training colours of overall Glossy Insignia White with Fluorescent Red Orange (commonly known as dayglo) trim

The L-245 was known at Burbank as the 'Lockheed Trainer' or T-33B, but this was unofficial since the project was being funded by the company and not the military. Completed in November 1953, the airplane was given the civil registration N125D and finished in a pleasing civilian scheme. After the first flight (which took place on 16 December 1953 from Burbank), some modifications had to be quickly undertaken. The raised and bulged canopy disturbed the airflow over the vertical tail resulting in poor rudder control. A large dorsal fin/spine was added by Johnson to get rid of this undesirable effect and became one of the main identifying features of production aircraft. Powered by an Allison J33-A-16A of 5400 lbs static thrust, demonstration and testing began to take place almost immediately. A foggy day at NAS Miramar nicely sets off this brightly finished T-1A (BuNo 144150) which was in use, during May 1964, as a station hack

Above Lockheed had been overwhelmed by the success of the also privately-funded T-33A. Unfortunately, they were probably equally set back when the USAF showed absolutely no interest in the L-245. They hoped the USAF would view the L-245 as a follow-on to the T-Bird but USAF officials were perfectly happy with the T-33A, and fairly rightly so since the aircraft did perform its mission in a cost-efficient manner. However, the US Navy liked the idea of the lower speeds (extremely useful for training carrier pilots) and felt the L-245 might make an ideal jet trainer for landing on carriers. Accordingly, in May 1954, a contract was issued to Lockheed for the production of eight T2V-1 aircraft. Power would be an uprated Allison J33-A-24 or -24A of 6100 lbs thrust. The new aircraft was assigned Lockheed Model Number 1080-91-08 while the Navy assigned BuNos 142261 through 142268. T-1A BuNo 144147 was with H&MS-32 in March 1968 and is wearing a very faded and patched scheme of overall Aircraft Gray

Overleaf A rather revolutionary feature of the L-245 was the incorporation of boundary layer control (BLC) which used compressed air, bled from the compression chambers of the jet, passing through slots and over the top of leading edge slats. This, Kelly Johnson hoped, would improve the new aircraft's low-speed handling characteristics. Johnson predicted that BLC would improve control while lowering landing speed by 4 knots—takeoff speed would be reduced by 7 kts when compared to a standard T-33A. Through a deal with the USAF, Lockheed purchased back T-33A s/n 52-9255 (c/n 580-7321) and set to work producing the L-245 prototype. Photographed during March 1965, T-1A BuNo 144750 is seen being towed out for a flight. Assigned to USMC MAMS-37, the T-1A is attractively finished in Glossy Insignia White with Fluorescent Red Orange trim

51

Data gathered from the testing of the modified L-245 was incorporated into the production line and the first T2V-1 began flight test on 20 January 1956 but it was to be a protracted period until the aircraft started carrier qualifications. In the meantime, the Navy issued further production contracts in four basic batches (BuNos 142397/142399, 142533/142541, 144117/144126, 144735/144764) that would bring total production to 150 aircraft (a further 240 planned machines were cancelled). Painted overall Aircraft Gray and assigned to USMC HS FMFPAC (WZ tail code, Fleet Marine Force Pacific) BuNo 144199 displays the non-jettisonable wingtip fuel tanks and the dorsal fin that distinguished the T2V-1 series

In order to make the new T2V-1 acceptable for carrier operations, Lockheed had to strengthen the rear fuselage and add an arrestor hook. The landing gear was also strengthened to handle the rigours of carrier landings, giving a gear that could take twice the sink rate of a standard T-Bird. The nose gear was made hydraulically adjustable so that the gear could be raised to improve the catapult angle from the carrier. The L-245 was accordingly modified as a demonstrator and was taken through an aerodynamic flight test programme at NAS China Lake where it was confirmed that the new trainer would be able to operate from carriers. T-1A BuNo 144171 carries the 7L tail code of the now (sadly) defunct NAS Los Alamitos in Southern California where the aircraft was part of the Naval Air Reserve Training Command when photographed on 11 January 1970

As production of the SeaStar (as the T2V had been named) got underway, Lockheed hoped to prolong the life of the type by proposing several new variants. Included among these new design proposals was the CL-330/CL-340, a stripped-down basic training variant of the T2V. The CL-341 was to be a transonic trainer for pilots transitioning to supersonic warplanes. Perhaps the most interesting of these projects was the CL-352 which was a lightweight all-weather fighter derived from the T2V (much like the F-94 Starfire which owed its beginnings to the P-80/T-33). The CL-352, if built, would have operated off anti-submarine carriers. The CL-352 would have been armed with either a combination of two Sparrows and two Sidewinders or two Sidewinders and two rocket pods. The aircraft would have had an estimated combat range of 580 miles and a top speed of 552 mph when fitted with a J33-A-24. This more prosaic and well-worn T-1A, BuNo 144212, was assigned to HEDRON FMFPAC when photographed on 14 February 1970

Above Well-maintained T-1A BuNo 142263 assigned to MCAS Beaufort and painted in overall Aircraft Gray. Limited production and maintenance problems saw the SeaStar withdrawn from flight-decks after the Navy decided that the North American T2J- (T-2A) Buckeye made a better carrier-landing trainer. SeaStars were bumped up a notch into the advanced trainer role

Overleaf Factory-fresh T2V-1 seen during a 1958 test flight from the Lockheed factory at Burbank. Never achieving anywhere near the success of the T-33 series, the SeaStar was even dropped from the advanced trainer role because the Grumman F9F-8T (a two-seat training variant of the Cougar) was available in bigger numbers, had the ability to carry weapons, and was an overall better aircraft. (Lockheed)

Left The first operational T2V-1s entered service in late 1957 at NAS Pensacola where its good handling characteristics were appreciated by instructors. A major set-back, however, was the BLC system which immediately began producing a variety of maintenance problems that were really never completely solved during the type's service life. The Marines took delivery of many T2V/T-1A SeaStars and the service usually operated them as hacks. BuNo 144163 wears the colourful Glossy Insignia White and Glossy International Orange (replacing dayglo) high visibility scheme. Photographed at Andrews AFB during April 1965

Below With its operating mission virtually eliminated, most of the SeaStar fleet was sent to Davis-Monthan AFB in Arizona for storage and eventual scrapping. T-1A 144143 is seen coated with protective material and standing in line with other T-1As while a row of T-33s brings up the rear. With no role for the SeaStar fleet, useful parts were pulled from the aircraft and the airframes were broken up and smelted down for aluminium and other metals. This SeaStar's last assignment was with the Navy's VT-10 training squadron

Silver Stars

Left Captain Martin Baggaley, VU-33, is seen in typical T-Bird pilot gear before an October 1987 photo sortie. Baggaley flies both the Silver Star and Tracker with the squadron. The bright dayglo markings are particularly useful in the squadron's primary mission and for the unit's secondary roles of fleet support, SAR, and target towing

Above *Finus Coronat Opus* (The End Crowns the Deed) is the squadron motto for Canada's VU-33, based at CFB Comox on scenic Vancouver Island. VU-33 currently operates four Silver Stars and three Trackers with a primary role of maritime reconnaissance. CT-133 133102 is seen over the rugged mountains that surround the large base

Overleaf Major Roger Arsenault, commander of VU-33, cruises past the scenic glacier that overhangs the town of Courtney, near CFB Comox. Major Arsenault's squadron comprises

12 aircrew, 54 maintenance personnel and two administrative clerks. Some of the pilots are dual qualified for the Silver Star and CP-121 Tracker

Preceding pages Major Arsenault rotates 133102 from the Comox runway. VU-33's T-Birds are getting close to an average of 10,000 hours flying time—with many more hours remaining. 'We feel the T-Bird is one of those aircraft with an infinite airframe life when properly maintained,' commented Major Arsenault. The CT-133 is powered by a Rolls-Royce Nene turbojet of 5100 lbs of thrust. Although an old technology jet, the Nene is quite reliable—being pulled every 300 hours for inspection and repair

Right All four of VU-33's Silver Stars and a Tracker are seen on the squadron's ramp area at Comox. All aircraft are flown quite regularly and perform useful tasks like target towing for live firing practice by the Canadian fleet. The dayglo paint really stands out. 'When the fleet is shooting at your targets, you want to make damn sure the aircraft is very visible,' commented one of the squadron pilots. Some of VU-33's aircraft carry a 'thimble' radome on the nose which houses an emitter capable of producing different Soviet and WarPac threat 'signatures'

Below 'Fill it up.' A T-Bird's tip tanks are topped off with, take your choice, 152 Imperial gallons *or* 230 US gallons *or* 872 litres. 'Depending on your age and where you were educated, fuelling sometimes takes a bit of headscratching,' said a T-Bird pilot

Far left The simple, by today's standards, front cockpit of the Silver Star

Above Silver Star 133119 carries the yellow and blue squadron colours of VU-33 on the rudder. The squadron was formed in November 1954 from what was known as the Royal Canadian Navy's VS880 West Coast Detachment. First equipment was the Avenger

Left Over the years, Canadian Silver Stars have worn a wide variety of markings. This view shows the maple leaf national insignia and the legend *Canada* proudly emblazoned on the side of the fuselage

Overleaf Large hinged dual nose panels give excellent access. At one time, two .50 calibre Brownings would have been carried in this area but most Silver Stars now have electronic gear installed in the nose compartment

71

Above New low-visibility paint on a VU-33 Tracker serves to highlight a Silver Star being refuelled

Right 'T-Bird break left now!' Major Arsenault banks away from the photo chase Silver Star. The underwing pylons that carry the target 'darts' are shown to advantage. In case of an emergency the large tip tanks can be jettisoned in flight. Aerobatics are usually not undertaken unless the fuel in the tip tanks has been depleted

Preceding page Another T-Bird break by Arsenault, this time in 'dirty' configuration

Overleaf The R-R Nene has proven to be a particularly reliable powerplant, which is just as well considering some of the harsh territory over which the Canadian Forces operate

Preceding pages Close-up view shows the new style of 'Canada' markings to advantage. There are several types of T-Bird canopies, some offering a bit more headroom than others. Considering the age of the aircraft, canopies are hard-to-obtain items. Over years of operation, each canopy has become 'fitted' to its parent aircraft which makes the fitting of a replacement a particularly difficult task

Left Unusual angle highlights the T-Bird's graceful lines and clearly shows the P-80 ancestry

Above Hydraulic pressure forces the dive brake full forward, and 133102 begins a rapid rate of descent

Above Nose slightly up, 133102 departs Comox after a touch and go. VU-33 pilots average 40 to 50 flying hours a month in a diverse number of military missions

Right Canadian Forces Brigadier-General Ian Patrick displays the Silver Star's classic lines over a low cloud deck near CFB Winnipeg during November 1987. This particular aircraft, 133398, is one of three Silver Stars assigned to

Winnipeg for general duties. Canadair constructed 656 T-33AN Silver Star Mk 3s powered by Rolls-Royce Nene engines. The company designation for the aircraft was CL-30 and the original Royal Canadian Air Force serials ran from 21001 to 21656 but when the RCAF was consolidated into the Canadian Forces, the new designation CT-133 was adopted along with new serials 133001 through 133656. Our subject aircraft was taken on strength (TOS) on 26 August 1954

Top left CT-133 (this designation has never really caught on with the Canadian pilots, the plane usually just being called a 'T-Bird') 133299 sits on a snow-covered ramp on 6 March 1975, ready for its next mission. Many of the Silver Stars had highly polished natural metal finishes but this practice has now been dropped since each polishing takes off a fine layer of aluminium and, thus, slightly reduces overall strength. Since Canada plans to operate the T-Bird until around 2010, such polishing could prove harmful! This aircraft was TOS on 13 May 1954

Bottom left Silver Star 21623 was, when photographed on 29 March 1968 at CFB Toronto, being used by CFB Moose Jaw as a hack. Over the years, the Silver Stars have carried a wide variety of markings as designations have changed and since military aircraft now have to carry dual English/French identities. However, the colour scheme has remained basically the same: Natural metal with dayglo tip tanks. 21623 was TOS on 17 July 1958

This page Silver Star 133353 (using its old serial long after the change-over had taken place) was assigned to No 414 Sqn when photographed on 15 September 1972 at CFB North Bay. The Black Knights of 414 use their T-Birds for the electronic warfare (EW) training role. TOS 24 June 1954

Below Certainly one of the most attractive of T-Birds, 21500 was TOS on 15 July 1955 and was the 500th Canadair-produced example. Seen at Nellis AFB, Nevada, on 26 October 1963, the T-Bird was assigned to the famous RCAF Sabre aerobatic team 'The Golden Hawks'. 21500 was one of several Silver Stars assigned to the team. Painted overall gold with a stylized red and white hawk on the fuselage, the airplanes were most impressive on the ground and in the air. The Golden Hawks were formed in 1959 and disbanded in 1963 after their 317th performance

Right When photographed during January 1973, 133490 from CFB Bagotville was surrounded by USAF McDonnell F-1001B Voodoos. During the early 1950s, Canada began to undertake the mission of training thousands of Allied aircrew along with its own RCAF and RCN personnel. In order to do this in an efficient manner, the RCAF obtained twenty Lockheed-built T-33As (RCAF s/n 14675 through 14694). Named Silver Star Mk 1, these aircraft quickly proved their worth and a licence-built variant of the T-Bird was contracted by Canadair for mass production to fill the training requirement. 133490 was TOS on 30 May 1955

Left With the R-R Nene at 98% rpm, Brigadier-General Ian Patrick lifts Silver Star Mk 3 133398 from the CFB Winnipeg runway for a photo sortie especially for this volume. General Patrick feels that the new Skyfox (see last chapter) would be an excellent aircraft for the Canadian Forces. All modification work could be done in Canada and the already long life span of the Silver Star would be extended even further. The Skyfox, the General thinks, would be an ideal cross-country IFR mount for CF-18 Hornet pilots—giving the training needed while keeping costs significantly down and preserving flying hours on the Hornet

Above Highly polished Silver Star Mk 3 (c/n T33-52, the Canadair construction numbers employed the last two digits, aircraft 001 through 099, of the serial and then the last three digits from 100 on) seen on the ramp at CFB St. Hubert on 27 September 1966. By November 1951, T-33A 51-4198 (given RCAF serial 14695) had flown with a Rolls-Royce Nene engine which, at 5100 lbs st, offered additional thrust over the original Allison powerplant. This aircraft was to form the basis for the production Silver Star which differed in detail only

Below General Patrick brings the Silver Star in close for some formation work while Captain Rodney Ward rides shotgun in the back. With around seventy airframes available for Skyfox conversion, the Canadian Forces could have a modern high-performance machine that would be capable of base defence—much like the British Aerospace Hawks operated by the Royal Air Force, but at a much lower cost

Right Going over the top in a loop. With its strong airframe and crisp handling, the T-Bird makes a very good aerobatic mount. However, care always must be exercised because the T-Bird can bite back—in an extreme sideslip, the tail can be blanked out causing the trainer to 'tumble' (*gulp!*)

With everything hanging down, General Patrick displays the Silver Star in landing configuration. The large round installation directly aft of the main gear doors is a receiver for ELT (emergency locator transmitter) signals that is fitted to some of the Silver Stars that operate in a search and rescue (SAR) role in addition to their regular duties. The first Canadair-built T-33AN Silver Star Mk 3 flew on 22 December 1952 with test pilot Bill Longhurst at the controls. Production of the aircraft continued through 1959, with 656 aircraft constructed. When originally built, the T-33AN could carry two .50 calibre Browning machine guns in the nose while underwing pylons could carry a variety of weapon options including two 1000 lb bombs or sixteen 5-in rockets. Today's survivors have had all this equipment removed. Production reached $1\frac{1}{2}$ aircraft a day by late 1953. Beech Aircraft in Wichita supplied 200 sets of wings to Canadair for the Silver Star programme

Top left Certainly one of the most spectacular colour schemes ever applied to a Silver Star, the T-33ANs assigned to the Red Knight were absolutely brilliant. In 1958, the Royal Canadian Air Force gave approval to the solo aerobatic T-Bird that would carry the name Red Knight. The main reason for this presentation was to carry the RCAF presence to smaller communities where the Golden Hawks (with their Sabres) would not perform. The Red Knight operated from 1958 through 1969 (by mid-1968, the T-Bird was replaced with a Tutor) and it is a bit sobering to note that during the Red Knight era, a variety of T-Birds were employed and 17 pilots utilized—three of whom lost their lives in Red Knight aircraft. CT-133 21574 was TOS on 25 January 1957 and is, today, a museum piece at the National Aeronautical Collection in Ottawa

Left As this volume is being written, some Silver Stars still serve with the Canadian Forces in NATO. What is interesting is that these aircraft have received low-visibility camouflage as has 133345 which is assigned to 1 CAG at Lahr, West Germany, and was photographed on 5 July 1987. This particular machine was TOS on 29 June 1954. (*Denis J Calvert*)

Above Canada, as part of the Mutual Aid Program, has supplied Silver Stars to Turkey, Portugal, Greece, France and Bolivia. Over the years, the Canadian T-Bird fleet has received many modifications and updates (one of the more recent being the replacement of the upper wing skins—those size 12 GI boots have done a lot of damage). T-33AN 21641, carrying the old RCAF titles and flag on the vertical tail, was photographed at Nellis AFB on 26 October 1963. This particular aircraft was TOS on 11 December 1958

Foreign T-Birds

Vast numbers of T-Birds have been supplied to overseas governments friendly to the United States. Some countries such as Canada and Japan (210 licence-built examples by Kawasaki) undertook their own production but most nations have been glad to accept airplanes straight from the States. Many of these T-Birds have been brought back to armed configuration with two .50 calibre weapons in the nose and the ability to carry up to 2000 lbs of underwing stores. The US government provided at least 1058 T-Birds delivered directly overseas while many more have been pulled from US stocks as needed. Thailand has been a big user of the T-Bird and T-33A-1-LO s/n 53-550 carries the checked tail band common to many Thai aircraft

Above One of the largest operators of the T-Bird in Europe was France's *Armée de l'Air* who received 163 T-33A/RT-33A aircraft and, later, 61 T-33ANs. Assigned to GE314, this T-Bird is seen at Chateaudun on 14 August 1975. (*Denis J Calvert*)

Top right With a background of USAF Super Sabres, T-33A 14044 prepares for engine start. Like the USAF, the French used their T-Birds for a wide variety of training and tactical interface tasks

Right *Armée de l'Air* T-Birds were pretty much similar to USAF examples except for the changing of some minor equipment and the marking of everything in French. Tandem ejection seats are housed under the large canopy, which is raised and lowered electrically. In an emergency, the canopy can be activated manually. 16768 is seen during June 1967 parked next to a *Luftwaffe* T-Bird

Above T-33A 53096 in typical *Armée de l'Air* markings which were fairly standardized during the T-Bird's French sojourn. The T-33A has a maximum speed of 600 mph at sea level and a cruise speed of 455 mph at altitude

Top right Engine bay open, T-33A 14044 receives maintenance. When the French retired the majority of their T-Birds several years ago, many were returned to USAF control since the planes were purchased from Mutual Defense Aid Program (MDAP) funds and had to be either scrapped or returned to the Americans. Some examples were brought to Britain and donated to various aeronautical museums. A few were transferred to other countries but the majority were broken up

Right *Armée de l'Air* RT-33A 41548 (the French serials reflected USAF serials, this aircraft being 54-1548). The RT-33A was built as a photographic reconnaissance variant of the basic trainer and was equipped with oblique and vertical cameras in a modified nose section. Related equipment was fitted in the rear cockpit as can be seen. Lockheed constructed 85 RT-33As, virtually all being supplied to foreign air forces for which the RT-33A usually became their first jet photo-recon aircraft

Above The modern day *Luftwaffe* was also a big user of the T-Bird (flying at least 192 aircraft). Although now retired from active service, the T-Bird is fondly remembered by *Luftwaffe* pilots—many of who took their basic jet training in Canada on Silver Stars. *Luftwaffe* 9434 also carried USAF serial 52-9967.

Below Power cart at the ready, *Luftwaffe* 9524 awaits its crew. Re-equipment of the post-war *Luftwaffe* started with North American T-6 Texans but quickly proceeded to more modern types. The T-Bird gave vital training to a new generation of German airmen (and some not-so-new airmen who had cut their teeth on earlier jet aircraft, notably the Messerschmitt Me 262)

Right Beautifully lit against a Turneresque background, this *La Force Aerienne Belge* displays its attractive tactical camouflage and dayglo markings. This particular example was photographed in July 1969 but Belgium received its first T-33As during 1954, at which time some *La Force Aerienne Belge* squadrons were still operating Supermarine Spitfires

Bottom right Almost all *Luftwaffe* T-Birds carried dull NATO camouflage but most also had a splash of dayglo on the tip tanks to help distinguish the training role. 9467 was also USAF s/n 54-1557

Guard T-Birds

Below Although the T-33 achieved its fame as a sturdy trainer that taught thousands of future pilots the art of commanding a jet aircraft, the aircraft probably became best *known* when hundreds were assigned to Air National Guard units around the country. Often gaily painted with bright squadron or unit insignia, ANG T-Birds went everywhere—if there was a small but essential part to be picked up, if officers

needed some flight time, if DACT manoeuvres had to be flown, then the T-Birds were launched. It would not be incorrect to state that during the 1960s and 1970s, ANG T-Birds could be found at almost every USAF or ANG base across the country. T-33A-5-LO s/n 57-613 is seen on a snow-covered ramp during April 1974 wearing an overall grey colour scheme and the rather simple markings of the Minnesota ANG. The aircraft is carrying large underwing chaff pods and the small travelling case on its centreline rack

Right T-33A-1-LO s/n 52-9839 was assigned to the Washington ANG when photographed during June 1968. Flying Convair F-102s during this time period, the 116th Fighter Interceptor Squadron's T-Bird carried the unit's insignia on the tip tanks

Left The Montana ANG's last T-Bird is seen on the Great Falls ramp during May 1987, after the type had been withdrawn from service and 52-9672's three fellow T-Birds had been sent to Mexico. This particular aircraft had been with the Montana Guard since new and the 120th Fighter Interceptor Group hopes to keep the airplane as a monument. Crew Chief Ron Halvorson had been with this aircraft since 6 February 1954!

Bottom left Here's 52-9672 some 23 years earlier when the T-Bird was photographed on 15 August 1964 on the ramp at Andrews AFB. As can be seen, the airplane was not as pristine as above—being finished in overall natural metal with faded dayglo drop tanks and large identifiers painted on the tanks

This page S/n 52-9672 once again, this time during May 1968 and looking a bit better. The metal has been brightened while the lower surfaces have been given a coat of grey paint to aid in maintenance and to minimize corrosion. Note the TA identifiers on the tip tanks. A blue and white tail band had been added at this point

Below Beautiful line-up of T-Birds belonging to the 119th Fighter Interceptor Squadron, 177th Fighter Interceptor Group, New Jersey ANG. As this is being written (December 1987), New Jersey is one of two ANG units still operating the fabulous F-106 but is scheduled to receive new fighters early in 1988, just about the same time the T-Birds are phased out. These immaculate machines are each painted in slightly different shades of light gloss grey (*Denis J Calvert*)

Above T-33A-1-LO 52-9329 was assigned to 'The Flying Yankees' of the 118th Tactical Fighter Squadron, Connecticut ANG, when seen during October 1968. Based at Bradley Field, Windsor Locks, the first post-war combat aircraft operated by the unit was the P-47 Thunderbolt and the 118th was the first ANG unit to receive Fairchild Republic A-10A Thunderbolt IIs, this occuring during summer 1979

Left With the uncompleted terminal building serving as a backdrop, T-33A-5-LO s/n 52-9456 is seen at McCarran Field, Las Vegas, Nevada, on 21 September 1962. Assigned to the 122nd Fighter Interceptor Squadron, 159th Fighter Interceptor Group, Louisiana ANG, the T-Bird is in very plain markings. The T-Bird was extremely popular with Guard units because of the aircraft's excellent reliability and, if the T-Bird did break down away from base, there was usually always someone who could easily work on the type

Bottom left With an immaculate Military Airlift Command med-evac C-118A in the background, T-33A-1-LO s/n 53-5325 prepares for engine start, ground power unit hooked into the recepticle on the right side of the fuselage. The T-Bird, seen during June 1968, was assigned to the 159th Fighter Interceptor Squadron, Florida ANG, and carries the underfuselage travel pod

This page Some T-Birds had extremely plain markings during various phases of their operational lives and T-33A-10-LO s/n 53-5959 is such an example. Assigned to the 175th Tactical Fighter Group of the Maryland ANG, the unit received T-Birds in July 1954 as the first jets to be operated by the State. Conversion to the jets took some time since Harbor Field (the unit's base) was too small to accommodate the airplanes. The T-Birds were initially based at Andrews AFB then moved to Baltimore's Friendship Airport after necessary airfield operations. Conversion to jets was not a simple process and took longer than usual since the unit had its Mustangs at Harbor, T-Birds at Friendship, and F-86Es at Andrews AFB. The Grumman HU-16B Albatross in the background was assigned to the 135th Tactical Airlift Squadron, Maryland ANG. Photographed during July 1964

Surrounded by a sea of dayglo aircraft, attractively finished T-33A-5-LO s/n 53-4901 of the Pennsylvania ANG waits at McCarran Field, Las Vegas, on 21 September 1962. As can be seen, almost every non-combatant aircraft (and many combatant) aircraft had some form of bright dayglo marking—a far cry from today's toned-down warriors. This T-Bird was assigned to the 146th Fighter Interceptor Squadron, 112th FIG, when the unit was operating F-102As

Being prepared for a DACT mission with the Convair F-106As of the 159th Fighter Interceptor Squadron, Florida ANG, this light grey T-Bird is seen on the unit's ramp at Jacksonville, Florida. The unit received its first T-33s in September 1954 in preparation for the arrival of F-86A Sabres one month later. In 1988, the 159th is one of the very few units still operating T-Birds, four being in service. (*Denis J Calvert*)

Navy T-Birds

The United States Navy kept a watchful eye on the USAAF's early efforts with the Lockheed P-80 fighter. Though its Corsairs and Hellcats were devastating the Japanese, the Navy realized that the jet age was just around the corner and made plans accordingly. Three P-80As were obtained by the Navy for testing and one was equipped with a tailhook for deck landing trials aboard the carrier USS *Franklin D Roosevelt*. This led, in 1948, to an order for fifty P-80Cs, designated in Navy service as TO-1s. These were used mainly for training, with sixteen being transferred to the USMC's VMF-311. However, the Navy's main interest was in the two-seat variant, the TP-80C, and the Navy placed an order for twenty-six TO-2s (soon changed to TV-2) and this was to be the beginning of a long relationship with the Lockheed Racer. This well-maintained T-33B was assigned to USMC HQ Washington when photographed at Hill AFB on 27 May 1973

Left Sun-bleached and well-worn, this T-33B last saw service with NAS Atsugi before being sent back as deck cargo to NAS North Island for a complete overhaul. Photographed in January 1970, BuNo 141494 still carries some of its temporarily applied preservation coating for the sea voyage. Once in Navy/USMC service, T-33Bs (the type's September 1962 designation) quickly went to other tasks beside the training role and became drone directors, drones, and hacks

Bottom left Here's another T-33B assigned to USMC HQ Washington. BuNo 138064 was photographed at Andrews AFB during May 1965 and displays the period's Glossy Insignia White and Fluorescent Red Orange colour scheme. For contracting purposes, the original Navy order was given USAF serials as well as USN Bureau Numbers. The first twenty-eight aircraft were delivered as TO-2s, later redesignated TV-2s and then T-33Bs

This page The Navy and Marine procurement of the TO-2/TV-2/T-33B series eventually comprised some 699 machines. Flight testing revealed that the type was not readily usable for the carrier training role but it was ideal for advanced and instrument training (the L-245 would be privately developed by Lockheed to overcome the carrier training problem). Painted overall Aircraft Gray, T-33B BuNo 139014 is finished in the dramatic markings of VX-4, the Navy's Pt. Mugu-based test and development unit, during May 1967

Left Interesting view of a bare-metal TO-2, BuNo 126603, on a test flight over the Pacific Ocean. Only a few of the TO-2s were delivered in a natural metal scheme. This T-Bird is equipped with two standard 165 gallon drop tanks attached under the wingtips, which later gave way to the centreline fuel tank. Since this airplane is in bare metal finish, it is easy to see the 38.6-inch plug inserted behind the intake in order to accommodate the second seat. The designation block on the side of the fuselage shows the USN BuNo but it also carries USAF serial 51-4000, since the aircraft were obtained under USAF contracts for the Navy. (*Lockheed*)

Above T-33Bs were rapidly assigned to fighter and reserve units as hacks since the type really did not fit into the Navy's training programme. T-33B BuNo 137987 carries a 7L tail code, meaning the airplane was assigned to NAS Los Alamitos, California. The T-33B is finished in the Glossy Insignia White and Fluorescent Red Orange colour scheme appropriate to the March 1965 date when it was photographed. It is interesting to note that this aircraft is being operated without the tip tanks—making for, according to most pilots, a very superior handling T-Bird

T-33B BuNo 138031 at NAS Willow Grove, Pennsylvania, during May 1964. The T-Bird carries the 7W tail code common to Naval Air Reserve aircraft based at Willow Grove. Note how the 'last three' of the BuNo is repeated twice on the tip tank, along with the base designator

4M tail code on T-33B BuNo 138054 is the code for NAS Memphis. When photographed during July 1968, the Fluorescent Red Orange (dayglo) trainer trim had been replaced with International Orange which held up much better to weather and did not need constant repainting

Skyfox

The most ambitious of all Lockheed T-33 modifications is, without doubt, the rather elegant Skyfox. Brainchild of aviation promoter Russell O'Quinn, Skyfox is designed to utilize the ageing, but useful and sound, T-Bird airframes around the world. Unveiled to the aviation press at Van Nuys, California, on 21 May 1983, the Skyfox Corporation presented a sleek aircraft in an attractive white and grey colour scheme that made seasoned observers think a bit before they realized there was a T-Bird lurking under that hi-tech exterior. O'Quinn

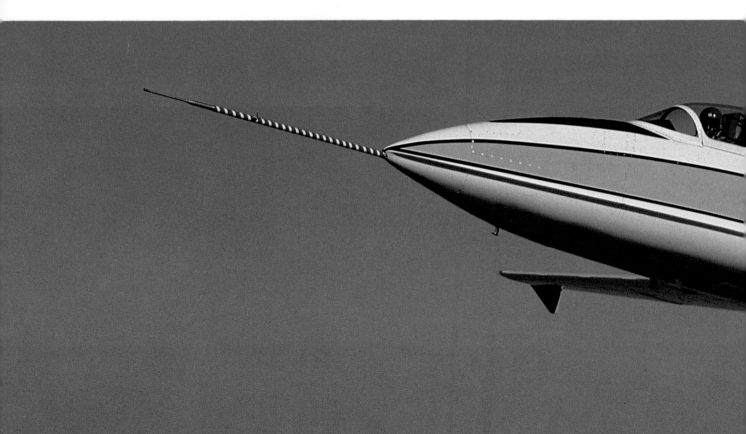

gathered together a pool of aviation talent (both designers and advisors) to help create the Skyfox including Irv Culver, designer of the T-33, and Tony LeVier, test pilot for the prototype T-Bird. Although Skyfox retains about 70 per cent of the original T-33 core, it really looks like a different aircraft

Part of the updating of the basic airframe included 'blending' the fuselage and wing, making a more harmonious join that improved airflow characteristics. With the engines placed on pylons, a great deal of room is freed in the fuselage for fuel, extra avionics, or, possibly, various types of aerial cannon. The Skyfox design hopes to provide, in a single aircraft, the capability of performing all aspects of advanced tactical aircraft training. That flexibility, combined with immediately off-the-shelf systems and already existing world-wide support centres, results in significantly lower Skyfox acquisition and training costs

Left Lockheed test pilot Skip Holm emerges from the Skyfox after an indoctrination ride at the airplane's Mojave, California, base during February 1984. At that time, the airplane was undergoing extensive flight testing at the Mojave Civilian Flight Test Center. The Garrett turbofans give the Skyfox a maximum speed of Mach 0.80 at altitude and 505 knots at sea level. The powerful, but fuel-thrifty, engines give a range of 3000 nm miles with no external fuel, a takeoff distance (over a 50 ft obstacle) of just 1010 ft, a climb to 30,000 ft in 5 minutes, and a touchdown speed of 95 knots. Skyfox can pull a steady rate turn at sea level up to 7.33Gs with power still remaining. At 36,000 ft, the airplane can pull a steady turn at 3.5G (buffet limit)—again with power to spare

Overleaf The most noticeable feature that distinguishes the Skyfox from stock T-33s is the propulsion system. Two Garrett TFE 731-3 turbofans each rated at 3700 lbs of thrust sit high on the rear fuselage. Skyfox Corporation anticipate a thrust growth to 4044 lbs for the Garrett powerplant. The original purpose of the Skyfox was, according to O'Quinn, 'to enable the world's air forces to counter the alarming trend in cost growth of newly manufactured trainer aircraft.'

Last page There are probably about 800 to 1000 T-Bird airframes around the world suitable for the Skyfox treatment. High airframe hours do not seem to be a problem, since the T-Bird is a tough aircraft and airframe life seems to be almost indefinite. Back to the future!